Healing from Emotional Trauma

Abuse, Rejection, Breakups, & Betrayal

Dedication

Everything I do and will ever do is for my three sons: *Julian Eli, Nathan Israel, and Christian Josiah.* You three are the light of my life, my greatest blessing, my hardest challenge, and my daily inspiration. I love you!

Mom

Jenny

Healing is a beautiful gift we give Ourselves.

Jessica

Preface

It took me many years to begin my journey of healing. I was wounded, scarred, and broken. I did not know how to love or let myself be loved. I settled for less each and every time. My self-worth and self-esteem were in shambles. I played the victim for far too long and lost close friends because of it. You see, it was more comfortable for me to live in pain than to actually be free. Freedom requires responsibility. Freedom requires making different choices. Freedom requires transparency. When I was tired of being alone, hurt, and feeling resentful, I sought freedom. I chased it down like a cold drink in a dry dessert. I needed it. I needed it in order to break unhealthy patterns. I needed it to be a better mother, daughter and friend. I needed it to live out the purpose in my life. Freedom requires forgiveness – a scary word for many. Forgiving ourselves and giving ourselves the GIFT OF HEALING is the very first step.

This book is not intended to excuse the behavior of those who hurt you or shamed you. It is intended to be used as a tool to *take your power back.* Whatever was robbed. Whatever was broken. Whatever was stolen. I want you to find the resilience and strength deep within you to *take your power back* and restore it all.

Welcome to your Journey of Healing...

Healing is a gift; we give
ourselves.
-Jessica Johanna

In this Book, you'll learn:

- Why forgiveness is crucial to your mental, emotional, and physical health
- How childhood beliefs can interfere with releasing the past
- You have the power within you to release the past
- Forgiveness brings freedom
- Strategies to assist you in forgiving and letting go

What benefits will I receive from this eBook?

- You'll learn why releasing the past is difficult and what you can do to make it easier for yourself.
- You'll learn the emotional, mental, and physical causes of your pain.
- You'll discover misconceptions about forgiveness.
- You'll receive specific strategies and exercises to assist you in letting go of your pain and moving forward toward the life you want.

Feel free to color in the pictures thoughout the book to help reduce any anxiety that may be triggered by trauma-related memories.

Introduction

Everyone has been hurt in one way or another. Some of us were hurt as defenseless children when a loving adult should have been protecting us. Others of us were hurt as adults by those who promised to love and care for us. Few people are able to let this pain go in order to move on with their lives, without the past hindering their joy.

I am not here to classify your trauma. If something hurts you, hinders you, and keeps you from living your absolute best life, then a root has embedded in your heart and it needs to be uprooted. Trauma looks different to different people. What is traumatic for one person may not be for another. I want you to know that your pain is valid. There is a reason for it. Your pain has a name. I also want you to know that your pain and the control it has over you, has the ability to be released and healed.

Some of us have a tendency to allow anger, pain, and resentment to control our lives. Many people do not understand that forgetting is *not simple* and that there are mental, emotional, and physical reasons why it is difficult to release this pain.

One area that can make it difficult to release the past is the misunderstanding about forgiveness. People often think forgiveness absolves the other person of what they did. You'll discover this is incorrect.

In this book, I speak about "your pain" or "the big hurt" in general terms, as I will be unable to cover each type of trauma individually. However, regardless of the cause of the pain, the feelings are often the same. Feelings of betrayal, shame, anger, resentment, hopelessness and disappointment. We may not have all experienced the same type of trauma, but we can all relate in one way or another to these same feelings.

I want to teach you strategies and exercises to release the past pain, trauma, and hurt. These activities range from recognizing your personal power, nurturing yourself, changing your thoughts, and discovering how to manage your feelings.

If talking about certain topics trigger unpleasant emotions for you, please take a break between chapters. This book is not intended to be completed in one sitting. Remember, Healing is a process, not a race.

So grab a journal or a notebook that you can dedicate to this process. Take your time; follow the prompts, answer the reflection questions, read the affirmations out loud, and most importantly, enjoy the journey ahead.

Common Reactions to Trauma

Re-experiencing the Trauma
Trauma survivors may re-experience their trauma through thoughts, feelings, memories, and other means. Re-experiencing a trauma can be very distressing, and may trigger uncomfortable emotions such as fear, anger, or sadness.

• Nightmares
• Flashbacks (uncontrollable vivid images and memories of the trauma)
• Distressing thoughts and feelings about the trauma
• Emotional distress or physical responses after experiencing a trauma reminder

Avoidance of Trauma Reminders
Because reminders of a trauma can be so distressing, it is common for trauma survivors to use avoidance to control these reactions.

• Using drugs or alcohol to suppress uncomfortable thoughts and emotions
• Avoidance of activities related to the trauma
• Avoidance of people, places, or things related to the trauma
• Suppressing thoughts related to the trauma
• Avoidance of conversations about the trauma

Negative Thoughts or Feelings
Negative thoughts or feelings may begin or worsen after experiencing a trauma. Some of these thoughts

and feelings might not seem to relate directly to the trauma.

• Excessive blame toward oneself or others related to the trauma
• Loss of interest in activities
• Feelings of isolation or disconnection from surroundings
• Difficulty experiencing positive feelings
• Loss of memory related to the trauma
• Excessive negative thoughts about oneself or the world

Hyperarousal

Reactivity, or a feeling of being "on edge", may begin or worsen after experiencing a trauma. This category includes a broad range of physical and psychological symptoms.

• Becoming irritable, quick to anger, or aggressive
• Heightened startle reaction
• Difficulty concentrating
• Frequently scanning the environment or watching for trauma reminders
• Difficulty sleeping
• Feelings of anxiety, and related symptoms such as a racing heart, upset stomach, or headaches
• Risky or impulsive behaviors

"Unlike other forms of psychological disorders, the core issue in trauma is reality."
— Bessel A. van der Kolk

Chapter 1
Understanding What Happens Emotionally

When you've been hurt by someone, there is more to the pain than "just" the one event. Emotions are a mish-mash of what has happened in the past, your pain in the present, your fears of the future, and your interpretation of what the event means about you.

Activating the Past

When you've experienced betrayal by someone you love, it hurts deeply. It hurts so much you wonder if you can make it past what happened. Sometimes that pain is about more than that one event.

If someone betrayed you, the pain for all the times you were betrayed is awakened:

- You may not remember the events of the emotions triggered but they are still adding to the hurt you experience now.

- When you were betrayed in past relationships, no matter how old you were, that pain is stored in your body.

- **Your emotions don't care about the actual event. But they recognize the pain.** The pain of the past is awakened and rises up adding to the hurt. It's like the pain joins together in one big scream.

It's difficult to release the past when it's like a tangled chain and the pain of every betrayal you ever felt is attached to it.

The Loss of Dreams

Every relationship, job, or activity you enter into has dreams attached to it. Some of these dreams are small, such as going to a party and having an enjoyable time. Relationship dreams are huge. Often, they involve plans for the rest of your life.

When a relationship ends, everything you thought would happen in the future ends:

- Your dreams of loving this one special person and being loved by them is gone.

- Your dream, your expectation, that you would care and support each other through the difficult times has dissolved.

- Your dreams of security, caring, excitement, and your idea of family have disappeared.

Your hurt is increased by the repercussions in other parts of your life.

Your financial situation may change, and your career be negatively impacted. Additionally, you may lose friends and people you considered family if you've lost your partner.

Each additional consequence of the initial event complicates the feelings involved. These additional hurts make it more difficult to release the past and move on.

No wonder letting go can be so difficult.

Loss of Your Sense of Self

It took time through the ups and downs of life to discover who you are. You may have felt comfortable with yourself and where life was doing and then "the big hurt" happened. Suddenly everything you thought you knew about yourself was shattered.

The ending of relationships is difficult. Ugly words are said, and accusations thrown about.

If you were in an emotionally abusive relationship, you have to sort through what your partner said about you and what you believe to be true.

If you entered the relationship with a healthy self-esteem, you may feel embarrassed and even ashamed of where you are now. You'll need to spend time getting to know who you are without your partner telling you lies about yourself.

Sorting through the negativity and finding the truth about you will be a challenge, but one which will have you discovering the wonderful and delightful you.

You may feel on unstable ground as you get to know yourself again. It takes strength and courage to uncover the self you think you lost. That strength and courage is within you waiting to be rediscovered.

When you discover that your relationship was based upon a lie, you need to redefine yourself and your relationship.

You'll feel the push to discover what is true and not true about your relationship. Part of moving on may be accepting you'll never know.

Before the big hurt, you may have defined yourself by your relationship. Suddenly that definition is no longer there.

Take time to discover the amazing person you are. Who you truly are is not based upon someone else's definition of you. Discover your own gifts and talents which are waiting for you to notice and use them.

You May Begin to Doubt Yourself

When you believe you've found the perfect person as partner or friend, and then that person leaves or betrays you, you begin to doubt yourself.

You may doubt your judgment. You may have thought you had good judgment about people but now you wonder if that's true.

It's not unusual to believe the fault lies with you. Yes, soul searching may be needed, but know that rarely are relationships all one person's fault unless one person has a mental or emotional disorder.

Your feelings about the relationship and about you are often deep and complex. This combination can make it difficult to release the past.

We'll discuss strategies to resolve these feelings in detail in a later chapter, so hang in there.

Summary

You've discovered that the following make it difficult to release the past:

1. Feelings from similar events increase the intensity of your feelings.

2. The loss of the future you dreamed about complicates your feelings of loss.

3. You may no longer know who you are, making it difficult to sort through your feelings.

4. You begin to doubt yourself.

Reflection Questions

To anchor in this chapter, please take the time to reflect on it and answer these reflection questions.

1. List at least 5 feelings you have about the pain you are feeling. List more if you can.

2. Write about how you've changed from before the painful event occurred to now.

3. How have your dreams for the future changed?

4. Do you have any doubts about yourself? If so, please list them.

Affirmation for Today
I am allowed to cry.

I know that crying can be good for me. I give myself permission to let my tears fall.

Crying relieves my stress. ***My tears help to wash toxins and stress hormones out of my body.*** I feel cleansed and refreshed.

Crying shows me where I want to make changes in my life. I look for the reasons behind my anger and sadness. I work at becoming more assertive or dealing with rejection. I find more constructive ways to handle situations that disturb me.

Crying gives me an opportunity to see that I have others who care about me. ***My relationships grow stronger when I allow myself to be vulnerable and accept assistance from others.***

Crying reminds me to treat myself gently. My life is precious, and my wellbeing is important. I accomplish more when I respect my limits and pay attention to my needs.

Once I find an appropriate time and place, I cry for as long as I need to. Then, I pick myself up and work on finding solutions. ***Instead of wallowing in my sorrows, I turn my tears into a healing force.***

Today, I allow myself to have a good cry if I feel like it. I regard my tears as my friends. When I accept my feelings, I can put them in perspective and move on.

Self-Reflection Questions:

1. How do I feel when I see someone cry in public?
2. Where are some safe spaces where I can cry in my daily life?
3. What is one thing I can do to comfort myself when I am sad?

"The conflict between the will to deny horrible events and the will to proclaim them aloud is the central dialectic of psychological trauma."

— *Judith Lewis Herman*

Chapter 2
Understanding What Happens Physically

Not only do your emotions from similar past wounds combine with your most recent hurt, but your body also has chemical reactions which make releasing the past difficult. Your emotions trigger parts of your brain and the body's stress response increasing the difficulty.

This chapter is to show you that your emotional pain has a physical cause and difficulty releasing it isn't a weakness of character.

Your Brain Reacts Immediately

When you discover you've been betrayed, rejected, or your loved one is gone, your brain and body react immediately.

Your brain activates a series of physical responses resulting in chemical production that affects your thoughts and feelings:

1. **Your limbic or emotional brain reacts to your emotional pain or trauma.** This activated the stress response producing fear and anxiety.

2. **Extreme emotional trauma can result in PTSD (Post-traumatic stress disorder).**

PTSD can make changes to the brain which can be long-lasting. The result is extreme emotional sensitivity affecting relationships with others, yourself, and your environment.

3. **Your prefrontal cortex, the thinking part of your brain, is stressed.** This makes it difficult to think clearly and may cause problems with your memory.

Emotional Pain Triggers Your Stress Response

Your body's response to loss and betrayal is ancient. You need people to survive both physically and emotionally.

Your body developed physical responses to help you stay alive. Many of these make it difficult to release painful feelings.

See how:

1. **Your stress response, also called Fight-Flight-Freeze, activates stress hormones:**

   - **Adrenaline, produced by your adrenal glands on top your kidneys, is released.** Being rejected, betrayed, or losing your loved one is certainly stressful.

   - **Adrenaline focuses your attention on the painful experience.** This focus makes letting go difficult.

- Norepinephrine, produced by the adrenal glands and the brain, is similar to adrenaline. Norepinephrine combined with adrenaline are designed to help you run away or fight to save your life.

- **The challenge with emotional wounds is that there's no place to run to.** You end up "stewing in your own juices," making it difficult to let go of what happened.

- Cortisol, activated by the brain and produced by the adrenal glands, is the stress hormone which does the most damage. It weakens your immune system, can mess up your digestion system, and can cause weight gain.

- These stress hormones can save your life when you need to react immediately, like jumping out of the path of a speeding car. With emotional pain, they interfere with your health and make it difficult to let go.

2. **Sex hormones are affected.** You might not think that emotional pain would affect your sex hormones, but it does.

- Estrogen increases in both men and women, making them more sensitive to stress. Since women have more estrogen to begin with, this affects women more.

- Higher estrogen levels in men lead to a decrease in testosterone.

- **High estrogen levels in both men and women lead to an increase in depression.** When depressed, it's more difficult to let go of the hurts and pains of the past.

3. **Neurotransmitters: Chemicals produced by the brain.** Your brain reacts immediately to every change in emotion. Your brain responds to your painful feelings by producing neurotransmitters which act with the other body chemicals discussed above.

   - Dopamine, when you're stressed, acts on the very front part of your brain (prefrontal cortex) and makes it difficult to think straight. When you can't think straight, you can't logically think through what is happening to you.

   - Acetylcholine can interfere with your sleep. When you can't sleep, you can't think well, you're more sensitive emotionally, and have greater difficulty handling the "ordinary" stresses of life.

   - Glutamate is crucial for your brain and your health. **When you have too much, which can happen with the stress of betrayal and rejection, depression can be one of the side effects.**

   - Gamma-aminobutyric acid (GABA) is wonderful for being calm and relaxed. When you have too much, as with extreme stress, the reaction is opposite, resulting in anxiety.

Summary

In this chapter, you've discovered some of the physical changes which occur during extreme emotional pain. These are changes you had no control over. Your body responded immediately to your emotional reaction to what happened.

The difficulty you've been having in releasing the past and moving forward is not your fault. You'll learn strategies to overcome what's happened in a later chapter.

Reflection

Before moving to the next chapter, spend a few minutes reflecting on how the emotional pain you've experienced affected you. Prepare for releasing the pain, by saying aloud the statements given. This prepares your subconscious mind.

For each question, think back to before you were hurt. Evaluate how much the following emotions have changed on a scale of 1 to 5.

1 - Not at all
2 - About 25% more
3 - About 50% more
4 - About 75% more
5 - 100% or more than before the hurt

1. Anxiety: _____

   Say aloud: Anxiety was chemically created by my body and I will be able to reduce it.

2. Depression: _____

   Say aloud: Depression was chemically created by my body and I will be able to reduce it.

3. Hopelessness: _____

   Say aloud: Hopelessness was chemically created by my body and I will be able to reduce it.

4. Mental Confusion: _____

   Say aloud: Mental Confusion was chemically created by my body and I will be able to reduce it.

Affirmation for Today
I give myself room to grow and heal from past wounds.

I validate my feelings about previous injuries, but I allow myself to move beyond the memories.

I understand it takes time to heal from injustices. I accept that my past wounds are a part of my being, but also that they are from events in the past. I can avoid letting them affect my present and future.

I clear my mind of negative emotions left over from past events. I forgive past injustices and those who hurt me. I meditate, pray, and even exercise to rid my body and mind of any stress.

My spirit remains strong despite the past.

I accept that life brings both positive and negative experiences. This acceptance enables me to grow.

Whether I am enjoying good times or life is less than ecstatic, I find the benefit from each experience. I make cherished memories in the good times. I learn life chapters and gain wisdom in both pleasant and troubling times.

Today, I am safe and whole. I have inner balance. I recognize my ability to overcome the past and look forward to a bright future.

Self-Reflection Questions:

1. How can I overcome my past wounds?

2. What can I do to avoid emotional triggers that set off memories of unpleasant times?

3. How can I find fulfillment through overcoming the past?

"We don't heal in isolation, but in community."
— *S. Kelley Harrell*

Chapter 3
Understanding What Happens Mentally

Now that you know what happens emotionally and physically when you've experienced the deep pain of trauma it's time to look at what happens with your thoughts and how you process information.

The Power of Your Thoughts

When you've experienced a deep emotional wound, the natural response is to attempt to make sense of it.

Your thoughts cycle through many questions, such as:

1. Why?
2. What did I do?
3. How could this happen to me?
4. Am I being punished for something?

These questions spring from the raw pain you feel.

It's crucial to realize that your thoughts are so powerful that they can intensify your emotional pain by increasing the production of the chemicals we discussed in the last chapter.

You've already been hurt by someone else. Don't make the pain worse by your own thoughts. Recognize the areas which can sabotage your healing and discover how to stop them.

Three Common Ways You Harm Yourself with Your Thoughts

You can bring healing to yourself through your thoughts, or you can make life more miserable. Do any of these apply to you?

1. **You keep thinking about what happened.** When you're caught up in the emotions and memories of an event, your subconscious mind responds as it did when the event first occurred. It produces the same stress hormones, creates the same neurotransmitters, and makes the same tracings in your brain.

   - **When you recall a painful event, you re-injure your brain.** Your brain and body respond just as it did when it first happened. Instead of being betrayed once, you are betrayed as often as you relive what happened.

   - **Find something wonderful and marvelous to think of** instead of reviewing the painful past.

2. **You make up stories to explain what happened.** Stick to the facts of the event. Don't make up anything as to why they did what they did. That just makes it worse. Unless

you were told, you just don't know.

- When you make up stories about what happened, you're also creating feelings, which has your body making all those chemicals, which then has you feeling worse, which has your body making more chemicals, which...

- **If you didn't see it or weren't told by the other person, precede your interpretation with "the story I'm making up is..."** This helps you realize that you just don't know.

3. **Your friends and family keep you stirred up.** You got to love them. Your friends and family want to support you. They may be angry about what happened and let you know. They need to heal, and you need to heal.

   - At first this is supportive. If it continues, your feelings are stirred up and you relive the event again.

   - **Use these strategies to help you and your loved ones who want to support you:**

   - Let them know how much their support helped you.

   - Tell them, in order for you to heal, you need to quit reliving it. They may ask how you're doing, but please don't rehash the story.

- Ask them to assist you by helping you to quit reliving the story. Give them something to say such as, "I'm glad to listen, but you did say you didn't want to relive what happened. How can I help you most right now?"

These strategies will assist you in breaking the habit of continuing to relive the painful event. Once you quit thinking about it, you can move back into happiness. (You'll learn more in Chapter 3.)

Summary

Your self-talk can support your healing or make it more difficult. Avoiding re-living the painful situation and asking others to not have you relive it will assist you in moving forward.

By managing your thoughts, you'll decrease the chemicals in your body which affect your attitude and mood.

Reflection

The following questions are designed to assist you in coming to know yourself better. Answer them as fully as you can.

1. Think back to someone who hurt you emotionally. How often did you keep re-living the situation? What did re-living the situation

do to you?

2. What kinds of stories did you make up about what happened? Explore the motives you attached to the other person and what you made up as their thoughts about you.

3. Consider a time the support of family and friends kept the pain alive. Explore how their bringing up the event either helped or hurt you.

Affirmations for Today
I am in full control of my emotions and thoughts.

I have the ability to direct my thoughts in any situation.

I choose to have thoughts that serve me. Negative thoughts create emotions and beliefs that are contrary to my purpose. I am always focused on my purpose. ***In every situation, I can choose to have a thought that serves me or impedes me.*** I choose to have thoughts that serve me.

By controlling my thoughts, I can control my reality. Directing my thoughts is easy for me.

In difficult times, I am focused on solutions. Only by thinking about solutions am I likely to find an acceptable one.

In pleasant times, I am focused on the experience. Allowing my mind to wander limits the amount of enjoyment I can experience. I am fully in the moment during pleasant times.

Negative emotions are signs that something needs to be corrected. ***When I experience a negative emotion, I immediately focus on finding an alternative to that emotion.*** This is the only time a negative emotion serves a useful purpose.

It can be challenging to control my thoughts and emotions. When my thoughts stray, I gently bring them back to the present. Life can only be lived and experienced in the moment.

Today, I keep my thoughts focused on the present. *I limit my mind's tendency to dwell on the past and wonder about the future.* I am in full control of my emotions and thoughts.

Self-Reflection Questions:

1. When do I find it most challenging to control my thoughts?

2. When is it easiest to control my thoughts?

3. How would my life change if I had greater control over my thoughts and emotions?

I can control my thoughts.

I take direct action to manage my thoughts. An important part of controlling my mind is the ability to stop unwanted thoughts. When I experience the same idea repetitively, I make a conscious decision to limit how long I will think about that topic. This way, I prevent my thoughts from tiring me emotionally.

Although any challenging event can trigger me to have recurring or troublesome thoughts, I usually manage my mind well. Calmly, I reflect on whatever the situation is that I am experiencing. My deliberations are focused.

I resolve any conflicts that come my way through effective management of my thinking. *I take control of my thoughts to minimize my experiences of uncomfortable feelings.* Then, I move on with my life and all its routines.

Each day, I tell myself that I can be successful at keeping my thoughts under control. I have been victorious in the past with managing my mind and I see triumph in the future as well.

Controlling my thinking brings positive energy into my life. I discover the rewards of peacefulness and serenity through managing my mind. My path is free of any constraints when I choose my own thoughts.

Today, I am content with life because I know I can control my thinking. I plan to re-affirm my goal to successfully manage my thoughts.

Self-Reflection Questions:

1. Do I have thoughts that I struggle to manage?

2. What are the specific types of thoughts I experience that are challenging to control?

3. How can I ensure that I triumph in my quest to control my thoughts?

Summary and Reflection

The key to healing from emotional wounds is to be able to release the pain from those wounds.

In these past chapters you learned there are three factors which make releasing the past difficult:

1. When you're hurt, your body responds by producing hormones and neurotransmitters which affect your emotions. You can become anxious and depressed.

2. The tendency is to keep thinking about what happened to you. This causes your brain to produce more hormones and neurotransmitters, resulting in greater anxiety and depression.

3. The emotions which resulted from what happened also continue the cycle.

To stop this cycle, you'll need to access your inner power, release the past, and form your new future.

In the next chapter, you'll learn that misconceptions about forgiveness, the releasing of the past, may prevent you from letting go of what happened and moving forward.

Reflection

Before moving to the next chapters, spend time reflecting on what you've learned and discovering how it applies to you. This will prepare you for moving past your pain and moving into the wonderful future awaiting you.

1. What are the recurring thoughts of the past you don't want any more?

2. Read each one of these recurring thoughts aloud and then say, "You're on notice. I don't want you anymore. You are going to leave now!"

3. What recurring feelings of the past do you not want anymore?

4. Out loud, tell each one of these feelings: "You are not going to be part of my life anymore."

"Some people cannot be cured, but everyone can heal."
Unknown

Chapter 4
What Forgiveness Is Not

The emotions, thoughts, beliefs, and chemical nature of your body make it difficult to release the past, to forgive. The memory of what happened will be with you. **The key to healing is releasing the anger and resentment surrounding the event.**

Even for the deepest of wounds, it's crucial to find a way to detach as much as possible from the pain. In most cases this means to move into a state of forgiveness of the one who caused the wound.

Many people are resistant to forgiveness because they don't understand what forgiveness is. Before you explore what forgiveness is, let's look at what it isn't.

What Forgiveness Is Not

If you're told that you must forgive someone to release the past and gain peace, you're likely to angrily reply, "It wasn't my fault. Why do I have to be the one to forgive?"

Within that reaction is the thought that forgiveness is about saying that the person who did the hurting has no responsibility for their actions and the consequences of their actions.

Consider these important principles relating to forgiveness:

1. **Forgiveness is not about the other person.**
   When you forgive someone, including yourself, you're not saying that person has no responsibility for what happened. Their actions caused pain and, yes, they are responsible for that pain.

   - Even if they completely accept the responsibility for their actions, that doesn't take away your pain. Even if they tell you how sorry they are 100 times, that won't take away your pain.

   - **You are the one who holds that pain, and you are the one who will need to let it go.** No, it's not fair, but it is true.

   - Forgiveness is completely about you. It's about your freedom, your peace, and your future.

2. **Forgiveness is not about staying with someone who is toxic.** A major misconception about forgiveness is that you then must be with the person who harmed you, even if that person is toxic.

   - You don't need to be with someone who emotionally, physically, or sexually abuses you, lies continually, is drunk or high much of the time, or steals from you, whether they steal things, your self-respect, or your dignity.

   - **You don't have to be friends with or spend time with people who cause you**

to feel terrible about yourself.
Forgiveness doesn't require this.

- Your job is to care for yourself and those you're responsible for. You can forgive the person, release the anger and emotional pain, and never see them again.

3. **Forgiveness does not mean you have to trust someone who has betrayed you again... and again... and again.**

- Recognize that many people have an addiction. This addiction could be to substances, shopping, sex, gambling, even lying. An active addict has characteristics which are part of the disease and you only see those characteristics when they're using.

- They lie even when the truth would do better. They're irresponsible. They'll take care of their addiction first and not pay attention to you. They steal. And they won't even notice when they've hurt you.

- There are also those who have personality disorders. They can ruin your self-esteem, cause you to doubt yourself, and convince you that what you know you saw or heard is not true.

- You may release your pain by forgiving them but remember who they are. They can't help themselves. Accept that and stay away from them if possible.

4. **Forgiveness isn't giving away your power or making you weak.** Making the choice to forgive someone is one of the most powerful things you can do for yourself.

Anyone can hold onto anger. Comparatively few can truly forgive. That is the topic of the next chapter.

Summary

In this chapter, you've learned the basics of what forgiveness is not. **It's the misunderstanding of what forgiveness is that blocks most people from attaining freedom from the deep hurts they've suffered in life.**

Before moving to the next chapter and learning what forgiveness is, take a few moments to anchor in what you've learned.

Reflection

Please answer these questions as honestly as you can:

1. What is your biggest concern about forgiving the person who hurt you the most?

2. Everyone has done something they are ashamed of. What is your biggest fear if you forgive yourself?

3. List all the reasons you have for not forgiving that one person who has hurt you so badly.

Affirmation for Today
I forgive everyone in my past.

I am able to forgive everyone that has ever hurt me. I let go of negativity from previous experiences and set myself free from the prison of grudges, pain, and anger.

I remove the bitterness from my heart and mind. Holding onto this pain is unnecessary, unproductive, and keeps me a victim of my past. I choose to move forward into a life without it.

I eliminate the desire for revenge from my heart as I allow God or my higher power to handle things instead. I feel that it is important to let go and make peace. I reject past pain and anger. I get rid of the blame without residual sadness.

I notice the lightness I feel after letting go of the past and the people from it. **I am able to find joy again because I forgive.**

I forgive myself, too. I get rid of the constant reminders of previous mistakes and errors. I do what I can to make up for my mistakes, learn from them, and move on with a lighter heart.

I acknowledge my feelings and forgive.

Today, I show forgiveness and move on from my past. I stop allowing the past to control me and my present. **I let go of it and the people who hurt me.** I get rid of the pain, sadness, anger, and resentment and replace it with new memories I can cherish.

Self-Reflection Questions:

1. How can I forgive people without letting them hurt me again?

2. Where can I get more help to learn forgiveness?

3. What can I do to make it easier for me to forgive and move on?

"Forgiveness is giving up the hope
that the past could have been any
different."
— *Oprah Winfrey*

Chapter 5
What Forgiveness Is

Now that you know that forgiveness isn't about spending time with toxic people or giving away your power, it's time to look at what forgiveness is.

Very simply, forgiveness is FREEDOM.

- Freedom from having what happened always on your mind
- Freedom the anger and fear
- Freedom from having to grit your teeth when you see them

As difficult as forgiveness can be, it lightens the load on your mind, brings peace to your heart, and frees you to move forward to the future.

Refusing Forgiveness Affects All Areas of Your Life

Holding onto pain and resentment has major negative effects upon you. You'll find you're easily distracted by the pain, and this limits your ability to be fully productive. You also miss the joys of life.

When you relive what happened, your body reacts as if you just experienced the pain. You feel like a victim and have difficulty accessing your inner strength.

Holding onto emotional pain weakens you. You are like the powerful elephant prevented from moving because it believes the little chain around its ankle controls its life.

Let's examine more deeply what forgiveness gives you:

1. **Forgiveness gives you the power to move into the future.** When you're hurt, no matter how badly, you can feel like you're carrying around a ball and chain. You hold it so tightly that you've forgotten how to release it. If you allow it, that wound can lock you into pain and keep you from seeing the beauty in life.

   - **When you release the pain, you unchain yourself and throw away the chain and everything attached to it.**

   - Your body responds with an "Ahhh" and releases energy. This allows you to make plans for the future and open your heart to reviving neglected relationships and meeting new people.

2. **No longer are you defined by your wound.** Forgiveness allows you to be the amazing, wonderful person you are. Before you release the pain from that terrible hurt, you're defined as the one whose partner betrayed you, or whose boss falsely accused and fired you.

   - Avoid being defined by what happened to you. Define yourself by overcoming what happened and being more successful and happier than anyone thought you could be.

- When you're not focusing on the past, you'll find your path to happiness, the gift and talents you've forgotten, and the strength to look fear in the eye and go right through it.

- The pain will have changed you, but when you release it, *you* choose to determine what happens to you, not someone else.

3. **When you forgive, the other person no longer has control of you.**

- When you don't forgive, the person who hurt you has control of you. They're on your mind, occupying your thoughts, sapping your energy, perhaps determining where you go, who you see and what you do... and they don't have to say a word.

- Enough of that. Choose to not let them control your thoughts and emotions. Letting it all go demonstrates that they can't control you. You control what you hold onto and what you release.

4. **You get to make the powerful choice of releasing the pain and moving into freedom.**

- You'll no longer be caught in victim consciousness. Victim consciousness has you believing you are powerless, making it difficult for you to take positive steps for the future.

- You demonstrate what a powerful person you are to let something go that many people can't. **It takes great personal power to forgive.**

- No longer will you be hypervigilant, fearing similar injuries in relationships. **Your true self will shine through improving current and future relationships.**

5. **Your physical health improves.** When you forgive, there are powerful changes in the body which lead to a healthier and longer life.

   - In the last few decades, biologists and medical researchers have discovered the power of the mind-body connection. They have found that holding onto emotional pain affects the body mentally, emotionally and physically.

   - **The Mayo Clinic, one of the premier medical clinics in the world, identifies the following changes with forgiveness:**

   - Lower blood pressure

   - Stronger immune system

   - Better heart health

   - Less stress, which improves digestion, sexual response, sleep, and more

   - Lower risk of anxiety and depression

   - Improved relationships, which is known to strengthen your immune system, increase the "feel good" chemicals in your body, and reduce stress

As you can see, forgiving someone is one of the most powerful choices you can make to improve your life physically, mentally, emotionally, and spiritually. This makes positive changes in your relationships.

Summary

Now that you know the positive effects forgiveness can have in every area of your life, the question you may be asking is, "How do I forgive?" In the next chapter, you'll explore various methods which have proven to assist in forgiveness. **The key is finding the one which works for you.**

Before moving to the next chapter, please spend a few minutes right now to reflect on and anchor in what you've learned in this chapter.

Reflection

1. Think of someone who has hurt you and you haven't forgiven. Notice what happens to your body and how your thoughts and emotions change. Now write about what you noticed.

2. Bring to mind someone you love and feel comfortable with. Notice the changes in your body, mind, and emotions. List what you've noticed.

3. What do you want to achieve by forgiving someone?

Affirmations for Today
Forgiveness is a choice that I commit to.

I know that I have the power to achieve whatever outcome I want. Once I commit to something, it is easy to accomplish. **Committing to forgiving others makes it a natural response whenever someone offends or hurts me.**

Controlling the actions of others is beyond my capacity, but I am able to choose my response.

I take a deep breath in the midst of an upsetting situation and think about my options. I choose to make my responses constructive and positive.

Whenever someone has a negative reaction towards me, I avoid thinking that I am at fault. I am kind to myself, which makes it easier to be kind and forgiving to others. How I treat myself dictates my response to those around me.

Forgiveness allows me to have a clear conscience and a life of little stress. Holding onto grudges is counterproductive because it eats away at my soul.

My family members and I have occasional disagreements, but I always remember to treat them with love. **Having love at the center of my words and actions makes forgiveness a natural response to our differences.**

Today, forgiving others is work in progress, but it is doable because I am committed to it. I believe that whatever I set my mind to is achievable.

Self-Reflection Questions:

1. What are some offences that I find it difficult to forgive others for?

2. How can I make it easier for me to forgive others?

3. What impact does forgiveness have on my mood?

Summary

Now, you know it's not true that letting go of the past, also known as forgiveness, doesn't make you a victim and doesn't mean that someone unhealthy for you must stay in your life.

Forgiveness benefits all areas of your life. Your emotional and physical health will improve. You'll be able to think more clearly and move into the future with confidence and joy.

Now, all you need to know is how to accomplish this healing and life-giving process. That's what you'll learn in the next chapter.

To prepare for what comes next, please take a few minutes right now to reflect on the following. This will prepare your subconscious mind for your next step into personal power.

Reflection

Allow yourself to answer the following as fully as you can. Write what comes to you. Allow your mind to flow.

1. When I am no longer saddled with the pain of "it," I'll be able to:

2. Write out why a future without emotional pain is better than feeling the way you do now.

Affirmations on Forgiveness
Forgiveness is a gift I give to myself.

While I may have been wronged in the past, I choose to forgive others. Forgiveness is a gift I give myself. By forgiving others, I become free of the past. I am then free to live entirely in the present.

Forgiveness sometimes seems like a gift I am giving to others, but it is really something I do for myself. Holding onto the past creates challenges in the present and future, so I choose to let go of the past and move forward without baggage.

I am grateful for the challenges of my past. These challenges teach valuable chapters that I can use in the present.

By forgiving others, I allow myself to fully engage in the wonderful aspects of my life. I choose to focus on the good parts of my life and to release the past. The past only has the power I choose to give it. I choose to be free of the past.

When I feel that I have been treated poorly, I search for the valuable chapter in that situation. Then I forgive and forget. I am mistreating myself when I hold onto a grudge.

Forgiveness is a way of showing strength and compassion to others and myself.

Today, I give myself a gift by forgiving others for their transgressions against me. I feel light and free as a bird when I practice forgiveness.

Self-Reflection Questions:

1. Whom do I need to forgive?

2. What would I gain by forgiving that person?

3. Can I let go of my negative feelings about that person?

Forgiveness restores my peace of mind.

When I forgive others, I also liberate myself from being weighed down by past events. I wipe the slate clean and start anew.

Forgiveness puts me back in control of my life. I focus on my own reactions rather than external events. My resilience increases as I become more skillful at dealing with conflicts and disappointments.
Letting go of resentments reduces my anxiety. I know from experience that I commit many actions for which I need to be pardoned. ***It is important to teach myself that absolution is possible.***

Most of all, I take pleasure in knowing that I promote healing when I make allowances for mistakes and misjudgments.

A tolerant attitude helps me to better understand someone who hurts me. They may be feeling pressured or experiencing great losses.

When I respond with kindness rather than anger, we all have the opportunity to grow.

Absolution becomes easier and more constructive when I accept accountability for my role in any clashes. I am honest with myself about my shortcomings.

Distinguishing between people and their actions helps me to protect my own welfare while turning the other cheek. ***I understand I can feel affection and*** *concern for others without condoning behavior that contradicts my values.*

Forgiveness becomes more automatic as I rejoice in the good feelings it brings.

Today, I throw away grudges from the past. I enjoy the peace of mind that comes with extending forgiveness.

Self-Reflection Questions:

1. What are the barriers that make it difficult for me to forgive?

2. How does forgiveness make me happier?

3. Is there one person I could choose to forgive today?

"Once you choose hope, anything's possible."
Christopher Reeve

Chapter 6
Recognize How Resilient You Are

The evidence that forgiveness is one of the biggest gifts you can give yourself is overwhelming. Forgiveness strengthens your health and brings peace to you in mind and spirit. You've also learned why forgiveness is difficult.

You can do this! You have everything you need within you to discover how you can release the pain and forgive. You are more powerful than you ever thought you were. All you need to do is access that power and bring it forward.

You Have the Opportunity to Access Your Inner Power

The power you have has nothing to do with how powerful you feel. Even those you believe have accomplished much in their lives may not feel powerful.

You feel powerful when you have control over your inner world:

1. When you control your thoughts, you control your emotions and how you respond in life.

2. When you control your emotions, you control your thoughts and your response to the

difficulties of life.

3. When you control the way you respond, you control your thoughts and feelings about the situation.

4. **When you control your thoughts, feelings and response, you're able to keep the situation from becoming worse.**

When you don't have inner control, you're more likely to have a tendency to say and do things you later regret. Learn from those experiences.

As you work with the exercises in the chapters that follow, you'll learn how to control your thoughts, feelings, and responses. You'll be accessing and using the amazing power you have within you.

These concepts are key. Keep reading them until you can repeat them without hesitation:

1. **Whatever happened to you does not diminish who you are.** Unless you suffered a severe physical injury, you still have the talents and abilities you had before the pain entered your life. If your life has been filled with challenges, you may not have yet discovered how amazing you are.

   - When you release the pain, you'll feel more "you" than you've ever felt. When your inner vision isn't distorted with the past, you can discover your gifts, talents, and inner resources.

2. **You are the most important person in whatever happened.** Your well-being, inner peace, and health are all that's important in this process. Focus on yourself and what you need to do to achieve that peace.

   - If you're concerned about whoever else was involved, put them aside as you work through the following exercises.

   - **When you release the past, you will have the strength and energy to handle whatever is awaiting you.**

3. **What you do and say is about you.** What the others involved do and say is about them.

   - Remember who is most important right now: *you.* Don't allow what others say to you or about you distract you from what's important.

   - If you have family or friends who believe they're doing you a favor by keeping you updated on the others involved, ask them to stop. What they're saying is not important, at least for now.

4. **Releasing the past may not be easy, but you can do it.** Whether you're building a skyscraper or releasing the pain of the past, all are accomplished the same way: step by step.

   - Although you know your ultimate goal, focus on each step and the rest will fall into place. **Make a commitment to yourself now to do the exercises.**

5. **You'll be redefining yourself.** When the pain of what happened has been with you a long time, you may subconsciously define yourself by your pain. Be willing to release not only the pain, but also the way the pain defined you.

   - **No matter what happened, you can be happy again.** No matter what happened, you can be successful again. No matter what happened, you can have a loving and fulfilling relationship. Yes, life will be different, but it isn't over.

Summary

You have within you the power and ability to achieve your desire to release the past. Make a commitment to yourself to do the exercises. The rest will fall into place.

Before moving to the next chapter, where you'll begin focusing your mind on letting go, take a few minutes to review and reflect on what you've learned about your power to release the past by forgiving.

Reflection

The following questions are designed to assist you incorporate what you've learned in this chapter.

1. Describe how you want to experience your inner power.

2. Why is it crucial for you to focus on yourself as you do the exercises?

3. How has what happened defined who you are? How do you want that to change?

"The wound is the place where the
Light enters you."

— *Rumi*

Affirmations for this Today
I train my mind.

I control my feelings, thoughts, and actions. I train my mind to stay strong and healthy.

I focus on the positive. I count my blessings and express my gratitude. When faced with challenges and changes, I remind myself of what I have to gain. When I run into setbacks and delays, I find something to laugh about in the situation.

I monitor my self-talk. **I reframe my doubts and fears.** I give myself credit for making an effort. I accept myself for who I am now.

I adopt healthy habits. I work at making constructive choices automatic.

I engage in activities that sharpen my mental skills. I study foreign languages and play word games with my children. I register for online courses and shake up my daily routines.

I take care of my body. **My physical wellbeing affects my mental strength.** I eat nourishing whole foods, exercise regularly, and go to bed early.

I stay connected. Spending time with family and friends reduces my stress. I learn by listening to others and sharing my opinions and experiences.

I live mindfully. **I help my brain to function effectively by organizing my schedule and minimizing**

distractions. I use meditation and prayer to help me concentrate on the present moment.

Today, I give my mind a workout. I maintain a positive outlook and cultivate the kinds of thoughts and behaviors that help me to succeed.

Self-Reflection Questions:

1. How do I define mental strength?

2. Where can I learn more about exercises that can help my brain?

3. How is training my mind similar to training my body?

My past is behind me.

I am free of my past. What has happened no longer influences my life. I can leave the past behind me and look ahead to the future.

At times, I may have failed in the past, but I am unburdened by these setbacks. I can see the future with a positive perspective.

I use my past successes to my advantage. If I am going to look to my past, I focus on my successes. This keeps my outlook positive and hopeful.

I maintain my strongest focus on the present. I live each day to the fullest and enjoy everything that life has to offer. Many exciting things are happening around me. I steal from my present and my future when I focus on the past.

I know that I am unable to change the past. People have acted poorly toward me. I have made poor choices. However, I am optimistic about the future.

The future can be whatever I choose to make it.

Today, I am giving up the past for the present. My mind is rooted in the present moment with an eye looking toward the future. I have a bright future and choose to forget the past. My life is looking better than ever.

Self-Reflection Questions:

1. How has my preoccupation with the past harmed me and my life?

2. What would I do right now without the burden of the past?

3. How do I allow the past to affect my future?

Chapter 7
Changing Lies into Truths

You learned in the last chapter that you have the personal power to release your emotional pain through forgiveness. All you need to do is follow the exercises. Take them one step at a time.

In this chapter, you'll begin your journey by aligning your beliefs to your goal of releasing all that pain. You'll do this by giving direct messages to your subconscious mind. This lays the foundation for the other exercises which follow.

Give Your Thoughts some Directions

You may not know it, but your subconscious mind runs your life. You know those things you do automatically? That's your subconscious mind at work making your life easier. Your subconscious mind can also make life difficult when it's working with outdated information. That information was great when you were a child. It may have been exactly what you wanted last week, but this week you need something different.

I often call the thoughts from our subconscious mind: **LIES.** Because the information may be old, distorted, or taken out of context. *Thus, it lies to us.* You can upgrade the lies in your subconscious mind easily by telling it the following:

1. How you want your life to look
2. What you want to hear from others

3. What you want to tell yourself
4. What type of feelings you want to have
5. What truth you choose to believe

Just like a software upgrade for a particular program, this upgrade is for a specific belief. You're going to be installing truths instead of lies. The truths you need to achieve your goal of eliminating the painful past from your life.

Changing Lies into Truths

There are two steps to changing your beliefs. The first is identifying the beliefs you want to change. The second step is deciding what beliefs you want instead.

In Chapter 1 you explored why it's difficult to release the pain from the past. This difficulty may be due to thoughts and feelings based upon beliefs about forgiveness. It's important to identify these old beliefs.

Examples of old beliefs to upgrade are:

- Why do I have to forgive? They're the ones who hurt me.

- If I forgive them, they'll have power to hurt me again.

- I don't deserve to forgive myself.

Determine Your New Belief

Identify the new belief you want as your upgrade. Your new belief is a variation of the opposite of the old belief.

Using the old beliefs above you'll want to upgrade to:

- Forgiveness is a gift, I give myself

- Forgiveness allows me to have control over my life.

- When I forgive, the one who hurt me stays out of my thoughts.

- I deserve to have the peace which comes from releasing the past.

You can also use these techniques as you repeat your affirmations. Installing new truths and combating old lies.

In order to combat a lie, you need a truth. Every time you find yourself speaking negatively about yourself - **STOP** - and say something positive about yourself. It is important to stop the cycle of installing negative beliefs or lies that continue to cause you to live in pain and shame.

It is so very necessary to be kind to yourself and speak to yourself as you would speak to someone you love. You probably do not feel much love for yourself. If this is the case, then speak to yourself as you would speak to a dear friend, your child, or someone you really care about.

Start practicing speaking to yourself using words of encouragement, praise, affirmation, acceptance, forgiveness and love. You deserve this. You have been hurt enough and you deserve to be free of the pain that often times, we inflict on ourselves, by re-living and reminiscing on the past.

In order to stop a lie quickly, you must have a truth ready. This can be a truth that you have written on your bathroom mirror or in your phone. It can be a bible verse, a quote or even the affirmations in this book. Have your truth handy, preferably memorized.

When the lie creeps in be ready to **SHUT IT DOWN** with a truth. Repeat the truth 5 to 10 times until the lie dissipates. Repeat this process until the truth comes automatically following a lie.

Reflection

Repeat these truths when a lie creeps into your mind.

I am worthy.

I am valuable.

I am special.

I am loved.

I am accepted.

There is a plan and purpose for my life.

My past does not define me, it empowers me.

What was done to me will not hinder me but push me toward my purpose.

I will use my pain for my purpose.

I will use the test I survived as a testimony of my strength & resilience.

I am not a victim but victorious.

I have faced great obstacles and have overcome each time.
I am still standing.

The strength within me is greater than what is against me.

The opinion of others does not define me.

I am on a *Journey of Healing* and it is a daily process.

I am not where I used to be.

I am not who I used to be.

I am determined to move past anything & everything

that tries to stop me.

I am humbled by second chances.

I forgive myself, love myself, and am kind to myself.

Summary

Now that you know how to combat the lies that attack your mind and self-worth. Let's continue learning how to *take back your power* and restore everything that was taken from you when we you hurt.

I am so proud of you!

"The greater a child's terror, and the earlier it is experienced, the harder it becomes to develop a strong and healthy sense of self."
— *Nathaniel Branden*

Chapter 8
Claiming Back Your Freedom

Now that you've installed beliefs in your subconscious mind on forgiving and releasing the past pain, it's time to use those beliefs.

The next two chapters address the two major contributors to your pain: thoughts and emotions. In this chapter you'll learn strategies to control your thoughts as well as a powerful "trick" to command you into thinking what you want.

Your Conscious Mind Can Be an Unruly Child

Your conscious mind is easily distracted. You have the power to get your mind to "sit down and be still." Although your subconscious mind is set with the new beliefs, it's time to train it.

It's time for the real YOU to get in control of the unruly part of you which enjoys running amok and causing chaos.

Try these tricks and techniques to get your conscious mind, your thoughts, under control:

1. **The trick of being two different people.** This is like having two parts of yourself battling for control. **You want your healthy self to win.**

Here's one way.

- Stand tall in front of the mirror. This is your strong and powerful self who knows that you can release the pain of the past. Look yourself in the eye. You're looking at the "you" who's in pain.

- In a strong commanding voice say, **"It's over. It happened in the past. It's not going to change. It's time to move on."** Of course, adapt these words to suit you.

- You might hear or feel this whiney little voice start to say, "But, I...," interrupt the voice and say in a strong voice, **"No, I don't want to hear it. We have a life to live. Now let it go."**

- When you command out loud, you're reinforcing the beliefs you installed in your subconscious mind. You're telling your subconscious mind, "Yes, I really mean that I am ready to release the past and move to a healthy future."

2. **Put all your thoughts and pain in a letter.... Then burn it.** Research shows that writing things out with pen and paper has a positive effect upon the brain.

   - **Pull out pen and paper and write a letter you won't be sending.** No one will see this except you, so have no worries about how it looks or how you spell.

- Write a letter to whomever hurt you. You can write to a person, to God, or even to the past or future you.

- **Put all your feelings into that letter.** Use whatever language you want. Make it as strong as you can. Put the letter somewhere safe for a day.

- A day later, pull the same letter out. As you read it, cross out words and make them even stronger. Let all your anger, frustration, and pain come out in that letter. Put it aside for a day.

- Same thing as the past two days. Put it aside for a day.

- Take the letter out. Read it one more time. When finished, say aloud, **"I release and let you go. You have no more power over me. Be gone."** Then burn it.

- This process engages both your conscious and subconscious mind. Give it a try, putting aside your doubts about whether or not it will work.

3. **Change your thoughts. Reliving painful events only reinjures you.** Have your strong powerful self who wants to be free of the past talk sternly, but lovingly, to the part of you who is hurting.

   - Say, "Stop it. We're not going there." Then say, "Remember, this is where we're going." Begin imagining in all the sensory

detail one of those wonderful images you
used earlier when installing your beliefs.

- Avoid the temptation to be frustrated when
  you "catch" yourself rehashing the past.
  You'll catch yourself earlier each time until
  you rarely need to speak sternly to
  yourself.

Avoid Allowing Others to Bring You Down

Friends and family may say or do things they believe
are supportive but don't realize they're triggering the
memories and feelings you're ready to release. When
that happens, it's time to take firm but loving action.

If it's appropriate, tell the person who's making the
comments, "Thank you for your continued support. If
you would, I'd appreciate you supporting me by not
bringing it up again. Let's just talk about how
wonderful life is now."

If their comments trigger the feelings, give yourself a
pep talk. "Shake it off. You're doing great. Let's go
over again what life will be like when this is gone."
Then review one of your images you used when
installing beliefs... or develop a new one.

**Always remember how amazing you are and that
you can release the pain and move to a happier
future.**

What Freedom Really Looks Like

I want to take this time and ask you: *What does
freedom look like to you?*

Healing from past pain and hurt is not a one-time deal, it is a lifestyle. It is something you intentionally and purposely seek on a daily basis.

Freedom requires responsibility - *accepting when you are wrong or have wronged others.* It requires transparency - *being honest about how you feel or when something does not "sit well" with you.* It requires making different choices - *thinking about how your choices will affect you and those around you.* It requires holding no grudges or resentments - *knowing when to speak and when to let it go.* When to let someone upset you and when to let it go for your own *peace of mind.* Freedom requires emotional maturity - *knowing when and how to react in a difficult situation.*

Many people believe they are ready to be free from the pain of past trauma, but they really are not.

Continuing to live in pain and bitterness is very comfortable. It allows you to make a lot of excuses and take no responsibility for any choices or outcomes. It is always easier to blame someone else for the way things *"turned out"* instead of accepting responsibility for your own shortcomings.
I will let you know now; it is easier to continue living the way you are living... but it will be one cold, lonely and bitter life. It will be a life with no joy or purpose. It will be an unfulfilled life where you continue to grasp for something, anything, but end up empty each time.

If you have children, it will carry over to them. You may be unable to give them what a child desperately needs - love, acceptance and praise. It may create an endless cycle of pain and meaningless routines, that may even pass down through generations.

Yes, it is easier to continue to live the way you are living but let me tell you the consequences are too costly.

I know that I began my healing journey not so much for me, but for my sons. They deserved a healthy and happy childhood. They deserved a healthy mother who loved herself and in turn could love them fully. Initially, I did it for them but as I began to heal, I understood that I was truly doing it for me, because I deserved it.

You deserve it too!

Summary

Congratulations on learning strategies in how to talk to yourself and change the way you think.

In the next chapter, you'll learn how to change the feelings which bring you down.

Before you go on to the next chapter, please take a few minutes now to reflect and anchor in what you've learned.

Reflection

It's time for action. Please do the following now.

- Write out the words you're going to tell your hurting self that it's time to move on to a better life.

- Now, go to your mirror and say what you wrote. Write down what you experienced.

Affirmations for Today
I have the power to change my thoughts.

My thoughts are under my direct control. When my thoughts are displeasing to me, I take control of the situation and redirect them. **I strive to maintain thoughts that are both helpful and pleasing to me.** I can choose thoughts that serve me.

Everyone has the power to change their thoughts. I am developing this skill and getting better at it each day.

When I control my thoughts, I control my mood and my actions. The thoughts I permit to exist ultimately determine my results. I consciously choose what I want think about. My ability to do this is growing by leaps and bounds.

When my thoughts are distracting, disruptive, or ineffective, I take control of the situation. **I consider which thoughts would be most beneficial and change the direction of my thinking.**

Once I choose a new thought, I can maintain it with minimal difficulty. My mind is strong and capable.

My thoughts can alter my circumstances. I can alter my life and my experience in the world by changing my thoughts. Thoughts lead to actions. Actions lead to results.

Today, I actively manage my thoughts. I only entertain thoughts that propel me forward in life. **I block negative thoughts from remaining in my**

mind. I control my thoughts and my focus. I have the power to change my thoughts in an instant.

Self-Reflection Questions:

1. When am I most likely to have negative thoughts? What have these thoughts cost me?

2. What are some positive thoughts I could have more frequently than I do now? How can I encourage these thoughts?

3. How can I strengthen my ability to control my thoughts?

My thoughts are under my control.

I am always looking for new ways to better my life and myself. Fortunately, almost everything in the world responds well to positive thinking. *I attract what I put out. This is why, regardless of what happens, I keep my thoughts under control.*

Because of this commitment to myself, I regularly practice meditation. There are many ways I do this: when sitting at a traffic light, waiting in line at the bank, and sometimes in a formal practice, where I sit for a while and watch my thoughts. This practice assists me in being aware of my thoughts, so that I can control them better and better.

The nature of the mind is to wander. But my mind does this because it is my ally, always scanning the horizon for potential danger. However, if my mind begins to focus on less preferable thoughts, I exert control over my thinking. I direct my mind to come back to the topic I choose.

I feel empowered by taking charge of my thoughts. Because my thinking is under my control, I know that I can make the best out of any situation and get what I want out of life.

Today, I am grateful that I know how to control my thoughts. I am confident that my ability to do this increases with time and practice. I commit to myself to meditate today to increase my mental control.

Self-Reflection Questions:

1. Does my mind ever seem to "run away with me?" Do I feel easily distracted?

2. What can I do to encourage my ability to concentrate?

3. Are there specific thoughts I would like to focus on more?

"Freedom is not easy, it requires responsibility."
Jessica Johanna

Chapter 9
Calm the Pain

Now that you've learned ways to manage your thoughts, it's time to gain control of your emotions. You took the first step in the last chapter. Thoughts produce emotions.

Most people are surprised when they learn they can change emotions. Sometimes it seems emotions "just appear." They are actually triggered. You have the power and ability to tame those painful emotions. The skills you learned in the last chapter have prepared you for this chapter.

Feelings Are Important

Before you learn how to change feelings, it's crucial to know that feelings aren't bad. **Feelings are a natural human response to what happens in life.** They are a signal of what brings joy and where you are hurting.

For example, if you're with friends and someone brings up getting married, you could recall fondly your own marriage, or you could feel sadness because you're not married and would like to be.

What may be happy to one person may remind you of someone or something painful. Knowing how to work with your feelings when this happens is empowering. **These feelings aren't bad; they're painful.**

The Role of Grief

Whenever you experience a loss, you move through the stages of grief. The loss could range from scuffing your new shoes to the horror of betrayal. The stages of grief are the same for both but more intense for the more painful and life-changing event.

When you scuff your shoes, you'll go through the stages quickly and, probably, once. When you've been betrayed, you go back and forth through the various stages with changes in the type and intensity of feelings.

The more deeply you've been hurt, the longer it takes to navigate the stages of grief. Be patient with yourself as you use the tools below to navigate through the feelings.

Take Care of Your Long-Term Health

When in the midst of the pain of grief, it's difficult to think about the consequences of your feelings on your physical, mental, and emotional health.

It's crucial for your long-term emotional and physical health to feel, work through, and release the feelings which come from grief. In cases of betrayal or the ending of a relationship, it takes time to navigate those feelings.

For your emotional, mental, and physical health, it's important to release the anger, anxiety, and despair which can accompany loss. The sooner you're able to do this, the more quickly you can move on to your new future.

Adapting What You've Learned to Release Destructive Feelings

Discover how to adapt what you learned in managing your thoughts to learning how to change your feelings:

1. **The Mirror.** In the early stages after someone has betrayed, abandoned, or otherwise hurt you, it's important to encourage and support yourself. **As you stand in front of the mirror looking yourself in the eye, say aloud to yourself:**

    - "Yes, this is terrible, but you will make it through this."

    - "Yes, (whatever you need to say about the situation), but you will make it through this."

    - **After about a month or so, change your messages to:**

    - "It's over. Let it go and move on."

    - "They're not worth staying stuck. Let's get moving."

    - When you do this, you are telling your subconscious mind, "Yes, I recognize this is difficult, but I know I'll get better."

2. **Put all your feelings in a letter.... Then burn it.**

   - Use the same process you used in releasing thoughts. This time, focus on your feelings.

   - When you're ready to burn the letter, say, **"I release this relationship, this situation, and all my associated feelings. I'm beginning a new life!"**

   - Remember to write long-hand and not with a computer. This method is an excellent way to get those feelings out.

3. **Change your feelings.** It doesn't matter where your feelings come from, you can change them. Learning to change your feelings requires some advanced preparation.

   - Recall at least three wonderful memories.

   - Write each one out in detail using all five senses. Get in touch with the feelings you had at that event.

   - When you catch yourself feeling miserable, tell yourself, "Nope, I'm not going to waste this time on feelings that make me miserable."

   - Immediately recall one of those three happy memories. Immerse yourself in that memory until the other feeling is gone.

   - Because of the way the brain works, focusing on the happy and wonderful feeling cancels out the unhappy one. **The**

**more you do this the more your brain is
trained to focus on the positive.**

Summary

As you learned how to change your feelings, you
noticed that the exercises were similar to the one of
changing thoughts. **Thoughts produce feelings.**

In the next chapter, you'll learn how to change your
behavior so you can release the past and move to the
future.

Before you go to the next chapter, please take time
now to do the following exercise to anchor in what
you've learned.

Reflection

Take the time now to write out the wonderful
memories you'll use to knock out the painful
memories. Put in as much sensory detail as possible.
Include:

- How it looked (colors, shapes)
- How it sounded (voices, music, people's
  comments)
- How it felt (your own feelings and how your body
  felt)
- How it smelled
- How it tasted (foods, drink, imagine tasting
  something there like a blade of grass)

1. Describe an event in which you were proud.

2. Describe an event in which you were excited.

3. Describe an event in which you were peaceful.

Affirmations for Today
I channel my emotions towards positive choices.

I embrace my emotions because they connect me to my true inner self. They help me honestly express how I feel. My feelings are an integral part of me.

Even when what I am going through generates negative feelings, I use my emotions constructively. It is easy for me to find solutions to issues when I am emotionally charged up.

Sometimes taking a moment to confront my emotional state is what I need. Giving myself that chance helps me to turn any negativity into a learning experience. When I view my feelings that way, I am able to make sound choices.

Today, I take hold of each of my emotions because they help to complete me. I am committed to using them to build a healthy and positive existence. My decisions in life are based on acknowledging and respecting my true self.

Self-Reflection Questions:

1. How do I make the necessary adjustment when I find myself caught up in negative emotions?

2. When is it okay for me to acknowledge that I am unsure of what decision to make?

3. What can I do to manage my emotions, so they are more positive?

I set myself free when I release emotional burdens.

There is so much to be said for freeing myself from things that weigh me down. **When I release emotional burdens, I feel like an uncaged bird.**

Emotional burdens come when I remain in a relationship that breaks me instead of building me. Although I sometimes feel the urge to keep going, I recognize the impact on my well-being.

Remaining in a toxic relationship affects my happiness and health. There is great value in deciding to draw a line for the sake of my own physical and emotional wellness.

When I hang out with friends who gossip and express desires for what others have, I feel unfulfilled. Negative energy dulls my spirit and moves me away from a great existence.

Saying goodbye to uncreative timewasters does my body, mind, and soul good. I feel like there is more space to make a positive impact on the world. When I focus on positive things like spirituality and physical wellness, I feel more accomplished. There is power in letting go.

I embrace the opportunities to be happy and at peace. Those are the times when I am able to live my best life.

Today, I vow to release myself of each thing that is weighing me down emotionally. My days are well spent when I make room for healthy energy. There is beauty in giving myself the space to grow in a meaningful and positive way.

Self-Reflection Questions:

1. What are some of the emotional burdens that I am better off letting go of?

2. How do I know when something is weighing me down?

3. Where do I go to be quiet and introspective?

"When you go through deep waters, I will be with you."
Isaiah 43:2

Chapter 10
Changing Behavior

By reading the chapters and doing the exercises, you have strategies to change the thoughts and feelings which resulted from holding onto the pain of the past.

The last area to be aware of is your own behavior. Repetitive actions become a habit. Habits are actions which occur without thought. Recovery from the past requires that you apply thought to your actions and behaviors.

Know the Definition of Insanity

If you want to buy a vegetarian meal but always go to the steak house which puts bacon into its vegetables, you're never going to get a vegetarian meal. Every time you go to that restaurant wanting vegetarian, you'll be disappointed. That's an example of insanity.

Insanity is repeatedly doing the same thing expecting different results.

If you continue to go to the same park you and your ex always went to, and you leave that park feeling down or angry each time, you're the living example of insanity. True, you may feel like you're going insane with all the pain you're carrying, but there's no reason to make it worse.

To recover from the painful wound you've experienced, it's time to embrace the challenge of finding new things to do, new places to go, and new ways of doing things.

From Insanity to Victimization

Many people are examples of the definition of insanity. They also begin to feel like a victim because nothing is working out for them. You may have felt like a victim when the relationship ended. **You don't need to remain a victim.**

What happens after everything pertaining to the relationship is over, is that you are left with a major challenge. That challenge is to pull yourself out of feeling like a victim and get back in touch with the amazing, powerful you that is hiding beneath all that pain.

You are the one who can pull yourself out of repetitive and non-productive behaviors and become the wonderful you.

Behaviors Can Trigger Thoughts and Emotions

Your actions can assist in your goal to release the past or they can hold the past firmly in place. It's crucial to be aware of what behaviors trigger the emotional pain. **Once you know your triggers, stay away from them.** That's more difficult than you think, but you can do it.

Find New Things to Talk About

Avoid talking about the painful event with almost everyone. Talking about what happened brings up the feelings. Confine your discussion about "the event" and the person involved to your therapist, coach, spiritual leader, or support group.

Best friends, family, and those who enjoy hearing gossip won't help you. Your friends and family want to give advice and support, but it may keep the pain going.

Someone objective assists in moving past the pain. They'll point out where you're continuing to hurt yourself and how to stop.

If you still have the need to "talk," use the releasing exercise where you work on the same letter three times and then burn it. Repeat that process as often as needed.

Go New Places

If you always went to Joe's Pizza, it's time to get acquainted with Penelope's Pizza. If you always ordered pepperoni and pineapple pizza, it's time to order a different kind. Better yet, go to a cooking class and learn to make something new and different.

If you always went to a particular movie theater or at a particular time, go to another theater, unless you only went to the theater for them. Then don't go to the theater at all.

You may wonder why you need to change the places you go. You don't need to change anything as long as they don't resurrect the pain of the past. If being there continues to hurt you, **quit doing what hurts.**

Music Is a Powerful Memory Trigger

As much as you loved that song you shared, it's time to let it go. The memories associated with it can resurrect the experience of loss quickly. This is true for any music. Find new songs about your new life.

Quit Attempting to Figure Out What Went Wrong Unless You're with a Therapist

It's natural to want to know what you could have done differently. To discover what went wrong, you often need a therapist or relationship coach.

Just remember that you can't change the past, but you can apply your new knowledge to change your future.

Summary

Congratulations on almost finishing this book.

You've learned what happens in your brain when you're hurt emotionally. You've also learned why forgiveness, or letting go, is important.

You now have powerful tools and tips to change your thoughts and emotions so you can release the pain as quickly as possible. Then, you learned in this chapter the importance of changing certain behaviors, so those thoughts and emotions aren't triggered.

Before you celebrate the completion of this course, take a few minutes to answer the reflection questions so you can anchor in what you've learned.

Reflection

Please write out your answers to the following questions.

1. What activities result in painful memories?

2. What can you do instead?

3. What are the qualities of the wonderful you that you're ready to find again? List as many as you can.

Affirmations for Today
I am free to create my own reality.

I am in control of my destiny. I am responsible for my life. I avoid blaming others for challenges. **I avoid blaming circumstances for the direction my life has taken.** I choose the path for my life with my choices.

I believe that my life is what I make it.

My version of reality exists within me. While others may have a view of life with fear and limits, my reality is different. **My reality consists of limitless opportunities.** I am in awe of the possibilities that exist for my life. I make a conscious effort to hold a perspective that provides me with as many options as possible.

I create a positive reality by freeing my mind of hate, fear, and jealously. I make room in my mind for positive thoughts and emotions. **Holding negative energy ensures that my reality is unpleasant.** I release negative energy and focus on the positive.

I accept the changes that naturally occur in life. Resistance is a waste of time and energy. I allow reality to be reality. **What I can change are the perceptions and beliefs I hold in my mind.** The external world is largely outside my control. This is fine, because my beliefs and focus determine my reality.

Today, I am making my strongest effort to create a reality that serves my life. I have the hope and ambition necessary to make positive changes in my life. I am free to create my own reality.

Self-Reflection Questions:

1. How do I get in my own way?

2. Which of my beliefs make it more challenging for me to be happy and successful?

3. What is my vision for the future?

I avoid self-pity.

I accept my life. When things go wrong, I stay strong. I avoid dissolving into a puddle of tears or feeling sorry for myself. I avoid anxiety and additional stress.

I understand that I am responsible for my actions.

When I make a mistake, I accept the responsibility and the consequences. I do what I can to correct the situation or make amends, learn what I can from the error, and then move on without worrying about it.

I am in control of my emotions. I reject the idea that I am a victim. I avoid negative thoughts and feelings and focus on the positive aspects of any situation.

When I encounter a challenge, I remind myself that such obstacles are a normal part of life, and work on seeking a solution. I know that I am a strong individual who is capable of overcoming obstacles.

I accept my circumstances - whatever they may be.

I avoid wallowing in self-pity if things go awry. Feeling sorry for myself is a downward spiral, and makes everything seem worse than it really is.

Likewise, I avoid seeking company for my misery. Instead of having a pity party, I take action to get past hard times on my own and move forward toward a brighter future.

Today, I avoid self-pity by focusing on the positive things in my life. I say thank you for everything that have achieved to this day. In return, I then receive even more great things to be thankful for.

Self-Reflection Questions:

1. How do I avoid self-pity when I am sick?

2. Is it possible to avoid self-pity when I feel stuck or challenged?

3. What can I teach my children about self-pity?

Letting go sets me free.

Holding onto the past undermines my happiness and productivity. ***Letting go frees me and allows me to achieve my potential.***

I accept that everything changes. I adjust my expectations and realize that relying on temporary conditions for security is pointless.

I remove the conditions I have been placing on my happiness.

I recognize that some events are beyond my control and accept that letting go is the best option. There are times when I lose sight of what I value. If I wait until the decision is out of my hands, I pay a higher price. By anticipating natural shifts, I make the adjustment easier.

I transform my intentions regarding my relationships with others. I care more about their welfare than how they make me feel.

I examine my thoughts and let go of those that are holding me back. I realize that it is more constructive to manage whatever circumstances arise rather than wishing my life was different.

Letting go is an ongoing process. Starting with small issues trains me to handle bigger challenges. Showing myself that I can survive without cable TV may inspire me to ride my bike to work instead of driving.

My heart is open to new opportunities when I let go. My future appears brighter.

Today, I am more determined than ever to be more flexible. I am ready to let go and start over.

Self-Reflection Questions:

1. What is one possession I could give away today?

2. How can I be content with what I have now?

3. Why does letting go prepare me to receive more?

Summary and Reflection

In these chapters you've learned the tools and strategies which will assist in changing thoughts, feelings, and behaviors which anchor in the past. You now know that managing those three things comes when you access your personal power.

As you use the strategies in these chapters, you'll find the pain lessening. Your mind will clear, and you can focus on what's important to you. You'll be able to move into your new future.

Reflection

Describe what you'd do in the following situations:

1. You're out to lunch and the person who hurt you runs right into you. Your gut clenches and feelings of worthlessness pop up. What can you do immediately and what can you do later?

2. You're at a party and someone speaks in glowing terms about the person who betrayed you. The old hurt comes roaring back. What can you do to release the pain?

3. After the party where someone was talking glowingly about the person who hurt you, you can't quit thinking about what happened. What can you do?

4. Your route to work takes you past a place that reminds you of "the big hurt." Each time you feel sad. What can you do?

"If there's life, there is hope."
Stephen Hawking

Recommended Therapy Treatment for Severe Trauma

I did not want to end this book without providing you with recommended clinical evidenced-based treatments for severe cases of trauma. If your symptoms are severe and persistent and keep you from functioning on a daily basis, it may be time to consider clinical counseling. Here are some recommendations for therapy:

CPT
Cognitive Processing Therapy

CPT is a specific type of cognitive behavioral therapy that helps patients learn how to modify and challenge unhelpful beliefs related to the trauma.

Cognitive processing therapy (CPT) is a specific type of cognitive behavioral therapy that has been effective in reducing symptoms of PTSD that have developed after experiencing a variety of traumatic events including child abuse, combat, rape and natural disasters.

CPT is generally delivered over 12 sessions and helps patients learn how to challenge and modify unhelpful beliefs related to the trauma. In so doing, the patient creates a new understanding and conceptualization of the traumatic event so that it reduces its ongoing negative effects on current life.

This treatment is strongly recommended for the treatment of PTSD.

EMDR
Eye Movement Desensitization and Reprocessing

EMDR is a psychotherapy that enables people to heal from the symptoms and emotional distress that are the result of disturbing life experiences. Repeated studies show that by using EMDR therapy people can experience the benefits of psychotherapy that once took years to make a difference. It is widely assumed that severe emotional pain requires a long time to heal. EMDR therapy shows that the mind can in fact heal from psychological trauma much as the body recovers from physical trauma. When you cut your hand, your body works to close the wound. If a foreign object or repeated injury irritates the wound, it festers and causes pain. Once the block is removed, healing resumes. EMDR therapy demonstrates that a similar sequence of events occurs with mental processes. The brain's information processing system naturally moves toward mental health. If the system is blocked or imbalanced by the impact of a disturbing event, the emotional wound festers and can cause intense suffering. Once the block is removed, healing resumes. Using the detailed protocols and procedures learned in EMDR therapy training sessions, clinicians help clients activate their natural healing processes.

therapy result not so much from clinician interpretation, but from the client's own accelerated intellectual and emotional processes. The net effect is that clients conclude EMDR therapy feeling empowered by the very experiences that once debased them. Their wounds have not just closed, they have transformed. As a natural outcome of the

EMDR therapeutic process, the clients' thoughts, feelings and behavior are all robust indicators of emotional health and resolution—all without speaking in detail or doing homework used in other therapies.

PE
Prolonged Exposure

Prolonged exposure is a specific type of cognitive behavioral therapy that teaches individuals to gradually approach trauma-related memories, feelings and situations. This therapy approach helps clients learn that trauma-related memories and cues are not dangerous and do not need to be avoided.

Exposure is an intervention strategy commonly used in cognitive behavioral therapy to help individuals confront fears. Most people want to avoid anything that reminds them of the trauma they experienced but doing so reinforces their fear. By facing what has been avoided, a person can decrease trauma-related symptoms by actively learning that the trauma-related memories and cues are not dangerous and do not need to be avoided.

This treatment is strongly recommended for the treatment of PTSD.

Safety

This book may have brought up a lot of unpleasant feelings and emotions for you. It is completely normal for this to happen. Always remember if you or a loved one is at risk of harming themselves or someone else, please call 911 or go to your nearest hospital's emergency room.

Your life matters and there is still so much worth fighting for!

Suicide 24-Hour Prevention Hotline
1-800-273-8255

Afterword

As you finish this book, please know your Journey of Healing just begins. Healing is a process and not a race. People, places and things may be a trigger for you and remind you of the past pain. Know yourself well enough to PREPARE beforehand. Use your affirmations. You must guard your mind and your heart from people, places, and situations that may trigger the past for you. It is completely fine to avoid people, places and situations that trigger you. You do not need to apologize for this ever. If you can, stay away from them. If you can't then PREPARE. You do not need to apologize for protecting yourself. Feeling the pain again does not mean you haven't healed; it just means you are human. Feelings are fleeting, they come, and they go. Healing is a lifestyle, a long walk along the ocean shore, something you must purposely and intentionally SEEK daily. Seek it today!

If you need additional support, I would be happy to help. Book a session with me by visiting:

www.MyLivingPurpose.com

Made in the USA
Columbia, SC
01 March 2021